I GOT TODAY

Nancy Stanton Kempis

Copyright © 2018 by Nancy Stanton Kempis.

ISBN   Paperback   978-1-951469-30-6

All rights reserved. No part of this book may be reproduced or transmitted in any form or by any means, electronic or mechanical, including photocopying, recording, or by any information storage and retrieval system without express written permission from the author, except in the case of brief quotations embodied in critical reviews and certain other non-commercial uses permitted by copyright law.

Printed in the United States of America.

To order additional copies of this book, contact:
Bookwhip Company
1-855-339-3589
www.bookwhip.com

CONTENTS

Introduction 1

Spiritual Enrichment 3

Life Can Change 9

Cancer 13

Nicotine 17

Distress 19

Promises of God Pertaining to Healing 21

Facing Financial Problem 27

God Given Gifts 31

The Armor of God 35

Daily Meditations 41

INTRODUCTION

After 16 years in remission, nothing could have been more astounding to me than to be told that the cancer is back and it is now stage 4 with bone metastasis. There is something about this disease that makes a person stagger emotionally and in spirit. It doesn't matter if you are a devoted Christian or not this disease can cause people to feel fear.

I am writing this testimony to inspire those who might be going through cancer in whatever stage or for those who might be in some kind of difficult or challenging situation. The promises of our Lord are dependable. Our God is faithful and His word is alive for those who trust in Him. My experiences are real and the faithfulness of God is real in every instance of my journey.

SPIRITUAL ENRICHMENT

Have you been hit with hard blows coming from different directions? What will hold up for you when life hits?

Matthew 6:33 "But seek first the kingdom of God and His righteousness and all these things will be given to you as well."

On the second year of my arrival in New York, I joined Shalom Outreach Ministries, AG/NY under Pastor Roel C. Tiongco and Pastor Alex Suarez. The year was 2009. I was still confronting the side effects of cancer medication and radiation treatment at that time and I could hardly walk. Today, I am so glad and very thankful to the Lord for leading me to this wonderful ministry and wonderful sisters and brothers in Christ where I experienced not only physical healing but most importantly I gained spiritual growth. I was barely in remission and I had difficulty walking at that time but Pastor Alex and Sister Estrella Suarez came to pick me up every Sunday to attend the church service. They attended to my spiritual needs by making sure that I can hear the Word of God until I have become accustomed to coming to church on my own. Pastor Roel and Sister Lisa also came for me despite their busy schedule so I can attend bible studies during the week.

Isaiah 41:10 "So do not fear, for I am with you; do not be dismayed, for I am your God; I will strengthen you and help you; I will uphold you with my righteous right hand."

Unknown to my spiritual advisers, I was suffering from serious depression but refused to see a doctor and took no medication hoping it will just go away. Sometimes, I zoned out of reality and could no longer remember anything. I could not recognize people and places and it lasted for about five to ten minutes and sometimes longer. One morning I took the bus to go to work but while on the way my mind became fuzzy and confused. I no longer knew why I was on the bus and I did not know where I came from or where I was going. Nothing was familiar anymore and I panicked. I cried most of the trip but the Lord never left me and He took care of me during my ordeal. The lady bus driver remembered where she picked me up and she just dropped me off back at the same place and explained what happened until I recalled why I took the bus. I stood there for some time crying my heart out in self-pity. This experience was repeated many times but I prayed and trusted God to protect me.

I was lost many times and found myself in unfamiliar places but God in His goodness gave me a friend who I called during those episodes of sudden states of forgetfulness. My friend would either instruct me how to get back or she would come to pick me up. She probably thought I was just so stupid to get lost around New York City every now and then or she must have suspected something was wrong with me but kind enough not to tell me and I never told her my problem either.

Sometimes, I had sudden, uncontrollable episodes of crying and I cried myself to sleep. Depression was taking over my life but I was determined to keep my sanity intact. If you get to the end of yourself realizing that God is your only way, you lean on Him. I did that when I realized that my strong determination alone will not defeat the enemy. I needed God in me. I prayed Psalm 91:1-2 from my heart every moment and trusted in His word.

Psalm 91:1 "He who dwells in the shelter of the Most High shall rest in the shadow of the Almighty.v2 I will say of the Lord He is my refuge and my fortress, He is my God in whom I trust."

One time, Brother Raffy Marquez gave me ride going home from church. I was seated on the passenger seat when on the way suddenly nothing seemed familiar and I asked Brother Raffy, "where are we going?" and he replied with a question, "this is the way going to your home, right?" I thought at that moment I just had to trust the man who has been giving me rides and control myself from showing signs of panic. I am not sure if he noticed my sudden confusion but I kept silent. That was a very scary episode of my life but as usual, I refused to acknowledge that something was wrong with me and did not even tell my roommates about my ordeal. I was constantly in denial so I kept this to myself for a long time. I just continued to attend church services and bible studies and filled myself with the promises of God pertaining to healing.

I just realized much later that I was no longer in pain when walking. Not only that I can walk normally again but I also experienced emotional healing. The depression which I fought for so long just disappeared and was forgotten. During those seven years that I was with Shalom, I have filled myself with the Word of God and hungered for more biblical wisdom. It was a joyful experience that helped strengthened my faith and I learned how to trust completely in the Lord.

LIFE CAN CHANGE

~~~~~~~~

The Lord was merely preparing me during those seven years for a much greater test I would face yet in this life. The bible says, "Fear not for I will be with you," so I just rested in the promise of our Lord that He will never leave me nor forsake me.

Life can change at any moment for us. In March 2016, I worked as a companion to an elderly lady where I kept her company at home and wherever she went. One morning I went out to do errands for her. While crossing the street and pushing a cart containing two cases of bottled water, I was still in the middle of the street when the traffic light just changed, so I hurried, almost half-running. Suddenly the front wheels of the cart were caught in a deep crevice of the road and that sent me falling over the cart and I almost lost consciousness. The pain I felt in my right hip down my legs was so intense that I took a long time to recover. Two people who happened to be there saw what happened and came quickly to help me get up and walked me over to the other side of the street. Despite the resulting pain, I did not go to see a doctor thinking I will be okay in a few days. I had experienced falls in the past and I just got better after few days so I thought the pain will be over soon.

Days passed after this accident and instead of getting better, I felt that the pain was getting worse and every step was becoming so excruciating. It continued to worsen and by almost three months I still could not go back to work. By that time, I already needed crutches to get around the house. On top of this, I noticed that I was losing weight rapidly and losing my voice as well. Problems mounted on my head. I worried about my rent and my cell-phone bills, my insurance premium and other personal necessities. So I prayed to the Lord earnestly to come to my aid and show me what to do. And sure enough, the Lord answered.

The question is will you still have faith when things don't happen your way? Amazingly, God put me in a place where I was practically helpless, and I said: "Lord if this is the way my prayers be answered then so be it." I handed up the situation to God and felt a peace in my heart that surpasses understanding. I prayed and said "Lord, everything is now in your hands. I prayed Psalm 91: 1-2 as my mantra.

"He who dwells in the shelter of the Most High will rest in the shadow of the Almighty. I will say of the Lord, He is my refuge and my fortress, my God in whom I trust."

God will bring you to a place where you will be stripped of everything so you become completely dependent upon His will. There was nothing for me to do but to pray and keep trusting the Word of God and share with those who will listen. I believe God is God during the storm. He will bring you to the other side. He will make a way where there seems to be no way.

CANCER

It has been three months and my physical condition had worsened that I could no longer walk. I needed a walker which did not ease the growing pain and it already required that I should see the doctor. I was sent for X-ray and the initial findings showed and described my condition as "pathological fracture consistent with metastatic disease". Silently I recalled the horrible experience I went through sixteen years ago when I was diagnosed with metastatic breast cancer.

This is another proof that if you have Jesus in your life you have an enemy. The devil is relentless in his attack and he was there to deliver a hard blow. Deep in my heart, I trusted God knowing that the God I serve is greater than the totality of all of my problems.

Then I went for a total body scan and the result came out even worse. It showed cancer cells have spread all over the bones and across both of my lungs. I felt the complete absence of any kind of thought. I could not think and my head felt empty. All other problems were dwarfed by this report. I thought about my friend in Shalom who passed away due to cancer. I remembered somewhere in the past someone told me that the recurrence of cancer is deemed to be a life sentence. It was truly a numbing experience and I was in complete surrender to the will of God. It is when you let go of your problem when the hand of God continues to work on your problem.

Psalms 91:14-16 because he loves me, sayeth the Lord I will rescue him, I will protect him for he acknowledges my Name. He will call upon me and I will answer him. I will be with him in trouble. I will deliver him and honor him. With long life will I satisfy him and show him my salvation.

Everything was happening so fast and I found myself sitting in that tiny clinic and listening to the oncologist discuss treatment options for stage 4 metastatic breast cancer. I was calm and I kept on asking questions about the treatment trying to understand how different options work. At the end of our conversation, the doctor told me that in reality there is no real cure at this late stage. What the medication does is only to manage and control the spread of the disease.

Despite the hopelessness of the situation we were discussing, I felt only peace inside of me. I clung to my faith that my God heals and it is written in Matthew 8: 17 that Jesus fulfilled what was spoken through the prophet Isaiah. "He took up our infirmities and carried our diseases."

NICOTINE

The doctor turned the monitor and showed me the picture of my lungs where the cancer cells are and my eyes almost popped out of their sockets. She asked me if I ever smoked, I flatly answered no. There were two black spots dark enough for me to ask. "Are those holes?" believing those were cancer cells. She said no, that's nicotine. BAAM! That was a jaw-dropping embarrassing moment. During that meeting I learned an important lesson, never lie to your doctor. I lamely told the doctor the truth: I started smoking when I was 22 years old because of mere influence from peers and continued smoking for 18 years until I stopped many years ago, in 1994.

What the doctor said was so astonishing. She explained that the nicotine never leaves our system. It sticks to the walls of the lungs and causes lung disease and usually cancer. At that moment I was looking at the proof and could say nothing else.

DISTRESS

Being told you have stage-4 cancer could give you an unpleasant feeling that may cause problems as you cope with the disease and the treatment. It affects the family members and it can make it harder to deal with the changes that come with the diagnosis. I experienced different feelings throughout this ordeal ranging from sadness, uncertainty, powerlessness in my situation, and a feeling of anxiety. All these feelings can also affect how you think, what you do, and how you interact with others. I worried about my children and my husband, how they will cope with cancer and the things that may happen. They too have fears about what the future will be like. Anxiety and sadness can overcome them if I showed signs of despair.

One of the biggest fears of a person with cancer is death. I must think and believe this is not true. After all, there are 14 million people alive who have had cancer, however, I kept remembering my friend Sister Verna. Still, it is normal to be upset when one learns one has cancer no matter how much progress has been made in treating it.

PROMISES OF GOD PERTAINING TO HEALING

Anyway, after the doctor showed me the rest of the CT scan pictures it was time to walk by faith and not by sight. My Christian faith had to carry me through the battle I had to face. I thank those seven years I spent with Shalom Outreach Ministries in New York. It was a season of maturing in the Lord for me and it left a vivid Word fit for this moment in my life.

John 15:7 "If you remain in me and my words remain in you, ask whatever you wish, and it will be given you."

During that kind of moment, you are being hit seemingly from all directions when you know what you really got. It is written, "out of your belly flows a river of living water". I held on and trust in this promise. I declared His Word over and over again. It gave me courage and strength to trust in His plans for me; plan to prosper me and not to harm me, plan to give me hope and a future. I said, "Lord! Give me 30 years more".

At that moment I was facing two kinds of truths and I had to make a choice of which one to believe. One truth is about the results the doctor is showing me and telling me there is no real cure at this late stage. But there is a higher truth that the name of the Lord Jesus Christ is above all names as written in the book of Philippians 2:9

I said therefore, "in the name of Jesus Christ, stage 4 Cancer bow and be gone. I believe the Name of Jesus. I believe in the power of the name of Jesus mightily above stage 4 cancer".

It was time to cling to my faith, my only recourse to stay alive. The word of God just flowed out from within. "Is there anything too hard for the Lord?" Gen

18:14 and God said this to Abraham when the Lord blessed him with a son. I also remembered that the Lord said this to **Jeremiah 32:27 I am the Lord the God of all mankind, is anything too hard for me?** So I asked the Lord He bless me for 30 more years of restored good health.

Jeremiah 32:42 "This is what the Lord says: As I have brought all these great calamities on this people, so I will give them all the prosperity I have promised them." Then you can read all the promises of blessings and at the end the Lord said **"because I will restore their fortunes."**

I believe that God knows the plans He has for me, I trust his plans to prosper me and not to harm me, plans to give me hope and a future.

I asked myself over and over again. "Is stage 4 cancer too hard for the Lord?"

Jeremiah 33:3 says "Call unto me and I will answer thee and show you great and mighty things (unsearchable) you do not know."

I just kept on declaring the Word of God. I believe that my word is a tool to change my circumstances and to change my life.

Jesus said, "The words I have spoken to you they are spirit and they are life." John wrote in his epistle "In the beginning was the Word, the Word was with God, and the Word was God."

Therefore, I just kept on speaking the Word. I stand on the promises of God that "by His stripes you are healed" so I say in the name of Jesus I am healed. I give all my trust in Him knowing that the very word I now speak is a spirit, I speak His Word. His Word lives in me. I say "be it done unto me according to your word." I learned this trust in the Lord while I was in Shalom. Every moment I thought of those seven years so precious to me.

Matthew 8:17 "He took up our infirmities and carried our diseases."

I cannot describe the pain I went through every time it came. I turned to the Lord each time I went through it. When morphine was not enough or cannabis was not working, I would call on the Lord and called a friend to help me focus on the Lord and not on the pain. I thank all of those who prayed for me, the prayer group for including me in the weekly prayers, and most especially I thank my Pastor Rev. Roel Tiongco in New York who in most occasions even if he was driving he would pull over to the side to pray over me across America because I now reside in California.

Matthew 18:19-20 "Again I tell you that if two of you on earth agree about anything you ask for, it will be done for you by my Father in heaven; for where two or three come together in my name there am I with them."

Aside from the problems that cause much of the distress I had to deal with the side effects of cancer treatment. Every day I see my skin dry up, I experience fatigue, I have a problem getting around without a walker or cane. I wake up to tingling in my hands and feet.

Everything that happened this past two years made me understand the immense power of the Sword of the Spirit which is the word of God, and the power of prayer. I believe that persistent and consistent prayers accumulate and cause a healing breakthrough.

Every morning as I wake up I say "Thank you, Father God, I got today." I looked for improvements in my health. I thank Him for every little progress. I am slowly gaining my weight and regaining my voice.

I take joy in learning new skills to take control of my overall wellbeing.

FACING FINANCIAL PROBLEM

On top of all these surmounting problems, I haven't worked since I had the accident back in March 2016. With cancer the tremors became worse and so obvious that even aided by the walker I became so unstable and could not stand for a long time. I also lost my ability to write and was unable to carry things. My voice was gone and if it came out at all, I had to force it just to be heard or understood. Therefore, I had no means of earning to supply my very personal needs. Although my son is here to give me a roof over my head and food on the table, I still needed money for personal hygiene.

Romans 8:28 "And we know that all things work together for good to them that love God, to them who are the called for His purpose".

Psalm 34:4 "I sought the Lord and He answered me, He delivered me from all my fears."

By the grace of God, I am alive and well by the power of the name of Jesus. I have put everything in God's hand so all I have to do was find something I am able to do under the circumstance. I have to look at my situation from a different perspective. I am glad that during this very difficult situation, God granted another heart's desire to have the time to do what I love most to do without having to worry about anything else. This was a reminder to me that the Lord is ever present with me. The enemy cannot defeat me because I am a child of the living God. I know who I am. God is my healer and I have friends all over the world praying for me.

Now I can do crafting, crochet, paint and write. These things I have always hoped I could do and here is the most wonderful time to finally do it in God's time. I devoted my time to my hobbies wholeheartedly and by doing so my focus is no longer on my health issues and financial distress. I can remain positive despite the very negative situation.

Psalm 23:1 "The Lord is my shepherd I shall not be in want."

This verse in Psalms has been my mantra ever since I lost my dad to a motor accident when I was barely seventeen years old. Time and again the word of God had accomplished for me the full meaning of this verse. Having no income due to physical limitations was bearing upon me. God in His faithfulness shows up in my time of greatest need. I have been approved for early retirement and so all my needs have been met. My treatment continues at no cost. Every morning I wake up to the grace of God and I say, "God is good, I got today."

GOD GIVEN GIFTS

I am ever thankful that in my life I have learned and developed inner strength and persistence in the face of adversities and developed faith in the unseen God. I saw these important characteristics from my parents while growing up and realized that I had inherited it during my own life's tribulations. A person will never know what he's got until he has been tried to his limit.

There are many reasons we should not give up in the face of trials. I have four children who draw their strength from me as I drew strength from my own parents. I cannot show weakness and lose the fight. I persist to defeat the enemy the devil who constantly laid obstacles in front of us to steal our joy, steal our peace and destroy our faith. We cannot afford to give up our plans, our hopes and our goals because of adverse circumstances. God is just a breath away and He wants us to call Him.

Jeremiah 33:3 "Call unto me and I will answer you . . ."

I am also thankful that despite my simple life God gave me talents that serve me well in times of hardship. While I was in high school our family went through times of financial difficulties due to the growing needs of our large family. We were eight children all going to school. My contribution was making crocheted bedcovers, window curtains, valances and table runners for my mother's friends who were interested in crocheted materials. We sold a lot of them.

I have also learned beading gowns and formal dresses from my aunt while living with them for few years after my father passed on. At the time I was out of a job in New York and I supported myself through making beaded wedding accessories.

Now I have a physical condition that prevents me from getting a job, I turned to my hobbies again and learn new skills to keep me going in life. With friends who support me in prayers and patronize my painting and crochets, I count it all joy.

It is during this trying time when I draw out from within me strength through the abilities learned from childhood. By doing these I can explore more ideas in designs and uses of the items I make. This keeps me active and always positive and forward-looking. I leave no chance for negativity to invade my thoughts by keeping my mind filled with good ideas.

I plan far ahead and lift up that plan to God with great expectation. I refuse to entertain thoughts of dying anytime but instead look forward to the coming days when my plans succeed.

Proverbs 16: 3 "Commit to the Lord whatever you do and your plans will succeed."

My life is in God's hands but for as long as a new morning keeps coming and I keep breathing, I believe that God has a purpose for my life that still must be fulfilled. I will continue to share the good news of His promises. I will continue to make a testimony of His faithfulness the next thirty years I am asking of Him or until He comes again.

1 Peter 5:7 "Cast your anxiety on the Lord because He cares for you."

Psalm 55:22 "Cast your cares on the Lord and He will sustain you. . ."

Once you have cast your cares to our Lord Jesus Christ, let Him handle it. Do not take it back by worrying about it. The Holy Bible is filled with God's instruction to help us live a victorious life. All that is needed is for us to believe Him, accept His son Jesus Christ, and acknowledge Him as our Lord and savior. Then we continue to live a righteous life and declare His promises into our life.

We all were given a measure of faith. My faith cannot be greater than any others. We all were given the same measure of time. What matters is how we practice our faith to withstand the fiery darts of the enemy – whether in our finances, our health, our profession, and our loved ones. The enemy uses the things of this world to take us away from our faith in God. It matters how we use our time.

THE ARMOR OF GOD

Ephesians 6:10-13 "Finally, be strong in the Lord and in his mighty power. Put on the full armor of God so that you can take your stand against the devil's schemes. For our struggle is not against flesh and blood, but against the rulers, against the authorities, against the powers of the dark world and against the spiritual forces of evil in the heavenly places. Therefore put on the armor of God, so that when the day of evil comes, you may be able to stand your ground, and after you have done everything, to stand."

The succeeding verses 14 through 17 teaches us to have truth and righteousness, to be ready with the gospel of peace and in addition to these we must have a shield of faith, take the helmet of salvation and the sword of the Spirit which is the word of God.

Chapter 6 in the book of Ephesians in the New Testament is the best source of encouragement in times of trials. As we face difficulties it reminds us to be strong in the Lord and know that we worship a mighty God with mighty power. It also reminds us where the struggles are coming from. One may be struggling against the spirit of infirmities and diseases that causes a person to be sick all the time or suffer a lingering disease. It may be the spirit of poverty that causes your financial problem or losses in business. It may be the spirit of wickedness that causes people to do harm upon another or commit unlawful acts. The spirit of discord puts you in constant argument with another person.

Faith in God is most important when facing the enemy. When Jesus was tempted by the Devil in the dessert He fought by saying "it is written. . ." and quoted the word of God which is the sword of the Spirit.

The next verse 18 exhorts us to pray in the Spirit on all occasions all kinds of prayers and requests. Prayer is our way of communicating with our heavenly father. It is through praying that we can express our thoughts and emotions to our God.

Praying is fellowshipping with our loving father. Jesus taught us to pray daily when He gave us the correct pattern of praying we call "The Lord's Prayer". He also taught us to ask, to seek God and knock on the heaven's door as it is written in Matthew 7:7-12.

It is by asking we receive. I ask for healing every moment of the day and believe that He hears my prayer and that I am getting healed. My prayers get answered.

I also look back in the past when my requests have been granted. I haven't heard from my cousin since she left many years ago. Helen grew up with us and is more than a cousin to us. She is a sister in my heart I missed her so much. I prayed to God she will come back so we may see her again. I prayed for her every night before I went to bed until one day my prayer was granted. Helen came back and with her very beautiful children. We had a great reunion and I praised the Lord endlessly in my heart.

One day I prayed to the Lord and lay before Him the situation of us brothers and sisters. All of us were struggling in life and there seemed no light at the end of the tunnel for any one of us. I asked God, if at all possible, to change the direction of our lives for the better. It must have been my most fervent prayer yet so lacking in faith. Nevertheless, God granted my prayer so soon.

I was pregnant with my first child when we suffered a serious financial problem and I looked up to the heavens and said, "Lord, I forgive the person who caused me so much hardship due to a grudge that I am holding on to. Forgive me, Lord, and show me a way to get out of this hardship for the sake of this baby I am carrying with me." I praise God that He answered my prayers. We were able to start a business and as soon as my baby was born, blessing upon blessing came and we prospered so quickly.

There were so many answered prayers that I can look back on to encourage me to keep trusting and keep believing that the Lord is merciful and so good to me. He said He will never leave you nor forsake you and I testify on His faithfulness. He is Jehovah Rophe, the God who heals me.

As I lie down at night, I thank Him for the day and when I open my eyes in the morning I praise Him for the gift of another day; another day of joy, another day to praise Him, another day to declare His word.

The Lord said over and over again "fear not" so I no longer fear what might happen because I have submitted myself completely to Him to be healed and restored.

I hope this book will encourage you to keep believing, to keep coming to God for your worries, and keep on trusting in His word. Keep declaring his word of promises over your life for guidance, for healing and for the restoration of everything that you lost.

As I wake up in the morning I declare "I praise you, Lord, I got today."

DAILY MEDITATIONS

Ephesians 6:2-3 Who do you honor?

Ephesians 6: 14-18 – Stand firm

John 5:6 – "Do you want to get well?

John 6: 14 "Stop sinning…"

Hebrews 11:1 Faith

Romans 9:8 – God's children

Acts 17:28 We are God's offspring

Romans 10:17 Faith comes by hearing

Romans 8:34-35 – Jesus, our intercessor

Romans 8:26-27 – the Spirit help us

Romans 10:11 Trust

Psalm 73:25 Jesus

Psalm 42:1 – Desire God

Hebrews 11:6 – believe in God

Acts 12:5-7 – Corporate prayer

Romans 4:17

Manifesting the Blessings of God

3 John 1:4 prayer of intercession

Philippians 4:6 Do not be anxious

Psalm 37:4 Delight in the Lord

Hebrews 13:6 "The Lord is my helper I will not be afraid. What can man do to me?"

Proverbs 22:4 "Humility and fear of the Lord bring wealth and honor and life."

Psalm 18:2 The Lord is my rock.

Galatians 6:9 Do good.

2 Corinthians 3:16 In the realm of glory only the Word of God works

The Authority of Jesus

Mathew 8:23-27 – over the storm

Mathew 8: 28-32 – over demons

Mark 5:1-16 – over legion of demons

Mathew 9:1-6 – to forgive sins

Mathew 9:4 – to discern thoughts and intentions

Mathew 9:18-25 – over death

Proverbs 13:20

Hebrews 3:7-12 warning against unbelief

Romans 14:11 every knee shall bow

Mark 1: 41 "Be clean"

Other Books by this author available at Amazon and Barnes & Noble

Raising Adorable Children

Asdahlia-Child of the Sea

www.ingramcontent.com/pod-product-compliance
Lightning Source LLC
Chambersburg PA
CBHW030135100526
44591CB00009B/662